Help the Environment

Reusing and Recycling
Revised Edition

Charlotte Guillain

heinemann
raintree

Contents

What Is the Environment?

The environment is the world all around us.

We need to care for
the environment.

How Can We Reuse Things?

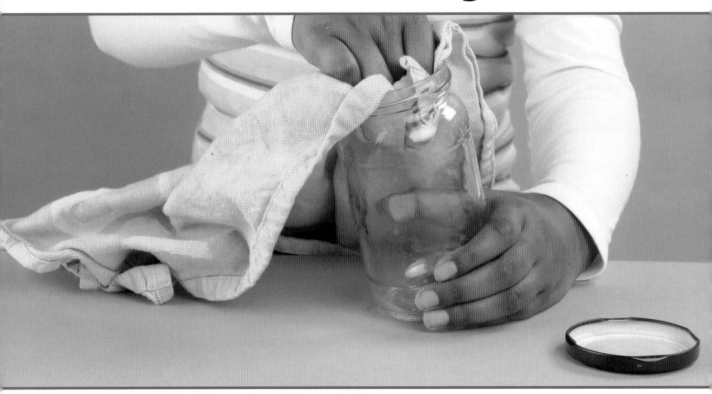

When we use old things
again, we reuse them.

When we reuse things,
we do not make trash.
We help the environment.

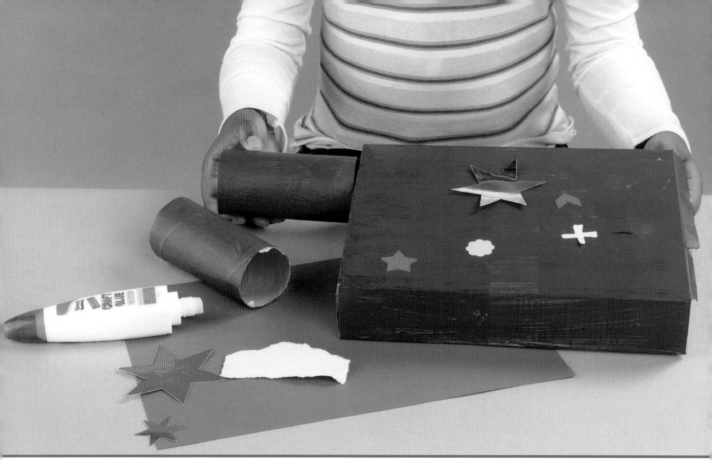

When we reuse boxes,

we do not waste boxes.

We help the environment.

When we reuse paper,
we do not waste paper.
We help the environment.

How Can We Recycle Things?

glass bottles

When we make new things from old things, we recycle them.

When we recycle things,
we do not waste them.
We help the environment.

glass

We use glass for many things.

When we recycle glass,
we do not waste glass.
We help the environment.

We use plastic for many things.

When we recycle plastic,
we do not waste plastic.
We help the environment.

We use paper for many things.

When we recycle paper,
we do not waste paper.
We help the environment.

We use metal for many things.

When we recycle metal,
we do not waste metal.
We help the environment.

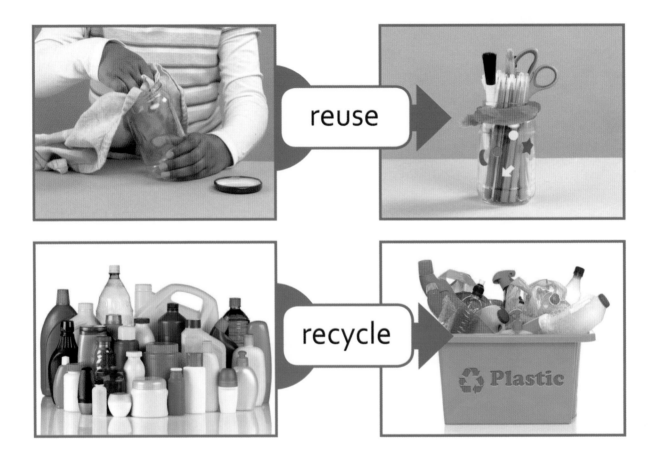

reuse

recycle

We can reuse and recycle every day.

We can help the environment.

How Are They Helping?

How are these people reusing things?

Answer on p. 24

Picture Glossary

environment the world around us

recycle make old things into new things

reuse use again

Index

Answer to question on p.22: These people are buying old things so that they can use them again.

Note to Parents and Teachers

Before reading
Talk to children about reusing and recycling. Explain how it helps the environment. Show them a sock that is too small for them to wear. What suggestions can they come up with for reusing (stuffing a soft toy, making a sock puppet)? Ask children to think about things that they can recycle, such as drink cans and paper.

After reading
• Ask children to bring in any material that can be reused to make something new (used foil, egg cartons,newspaper or used construction paper, fabric, etc.). Draw a very large outline of an animal, such as a lion or a dinosaur. Help children cut up some of the material and decide where to place it on the outline to make a collage picture.